House of Poems

House of Poems

by Donna Langevin

Wet Ink Books

First Edition

Wet Ink Books
www.WetInkBooks.com
WetInkBooks@gmail.com

House of Poems
by Donna Langevin

Cover Design – Donna Langevin
Cover Art – Seymour Skye
Layout and Design – Richard M. Grove
Author bio pic photographer – Brenda Clews

Typeset in Garamond
Printed and bound in Canada
Distributed in USA and internationally by Ingram,
        – to set up an account – 1-800-937-0152

Library and Archives Canada Cataloguing in Publication

Title: House of poems / by Donna Langevin.
Names: Langevin, Donna, author.
Identifiers: Canadiana 2025029589X | ISBN 9781998324231 (softcover)
Subjects: LCGFT: Poetry.
Classification: LCC PS8573.A55365 H68 2025 | DDC C811/.6—dc23

For My Readers

House of Poems is built from books instead of bricks. It is raised from the body of my own poems, and its roof is my second sky. Its spine lines up the courage I seek when fear or loneliness stalks me. It is peopled with memories of my beloved family and friends and contains my gamut of feelings for the unhoused. My *House of Poems* keeps changing place when I dwell in the hearts of others. This book is my "Open House" and invites you, my dear readers, to enter.

CONTENTS

Under the Same Roof

No Room Left

If I Were a House

Hark!

Galactic

Under the Same Roof

Under the Same Roof

For Richard

When we first married
we were so joyous you hung
a replica of Chagall's floating lovers
on our bedroom wall.

For seven years we flew without wings,
then without warning
your fiddle began to play out of tune,
our little blue boat leaked and sank
to the bottom of the sky.
The full moon fizzled out
as stars tumbled into mud puddles.

Dirty from affairs and cruel word-slinging,
we took down Chagall's *Bride and Groom*.
I donated my white wedding dress.
You quit wearing purple.
Though we no longer shared
a bed or our bodies,
I made you pots of lentil soup,
you baked loaves of rye bread
as flour clouds rose to the ceiling.

A decade later, I still darned your sweaters,
you patched my bicycle tires
and we took turns walking our dogs.

Holding your hand when you flew
from your sickbed into the cosmos,
I pinned the memory of those floating lovers
to a chamber in my heart.

Fragments

For Richard

I miss my poet's glass pencil jar
engraved with a plume and my name.
After you borrowed and broke it,
it left shards in my heart.

Today as I visit a potter's house
built from broken ceramics,
I picture you restoring these walls
after your seizures chipped coffee cups
and smashed our wedding gift platter.

I mourn my glazed horses
with lost legs and tails
after your elbow grazed them
and they leapt from the windowsill.

As I edge down the hall of this pottery house,
I recall the hand-painted plate you hurled
after you found my lover's letter.

Wondering why we lingered so long
in our shattered marriage—

Was it your porcelain promise to quit drinking
or the sunbeam that lumined the seams
of a clay goblet you mended?

Maybe it was the hours you spent
trying to reglue my bone-china horses
and your love that helped repair me
when I fractured my pelvis at the bus stop.

The Apple Gatherer

After a painting by Helen McNicoll, (Canadian) 1911

The apples you brush-stroked to life
bear no bruises or wormholes.
Dappled leaves, not yet tattered,
weave golden lace
across your model's white dress,
but the breath of autumn stirs the black
apron draped 'round her waist.

At age thirty-five, pursuing
the art you married
instead of a husband or child,
did you sense your season waning,
your palette, too heavy to hold,
choice of pigment darkening,
your thirst insatiable
as diabetes mottled your skin?

The light from your orchard spills over me.
I, who have lived long enough
to see saplings grow into trees,
taste my memories
of *Winesap, Gala and Granny Smith apples*
I savoured in pies, tarts and cakes—
sweets which harvested your life.

My eyes tracing the tendrils
and stems of your signature,
I join galleries of women gathering
what you called "apples of wisdom"
that Eve first plucked in Eden,
you hand down through this frame.

Under the Shadow of the Tent

After a painting by Helen McNicoll, 1914

Seated outside a large tent
shading the seaside beach,
Dorothea is opening her paintbox.
Marcella sketches driftwood with charcoal
while you, Helen, capture nuances of light
on their white smocks and hair.

Four decades later,
I slip through the frame
to join your friends.
Like you, I love those moments
when we're too absorbed in art
to worry about crafting word-necklaces:
sentences with missing beads.

Deafened by a childhood fever,
you listen with open eyes.
Stricken with my own family affliction,
I now hear the swish of an ocean tide
magnified by hearing aids,
but not the children splashing diamonds
or the screeches of gulls and terns.

At home in our silent realms,
you speak with paint.
My canvas is the page.

The Gleaner

After a painting by Helen McNicoll, c.1908

A big-boned farmgirl
with beet-red hands, sunburnt cheeks
and sweat glossing her forehead
hugs an armload of new mown hay.
Straw sticks to her coarse cotton sleeves
and flaxen locks tied in a bun.

Your own hair, Helen, sparse as dry stubble.
Painter's hand tingling,
did you ignore the way
your skirt hung too loose from your hips
when you planned that long trip
to render the seascape in Wales?
The one you would never take.

My DNR form, taped to my fridge,
power of attorney signed, I shiver
as the Harvester stalks me
just as he shadowed you
while you stood in front of your easel
dipping your sunlit brush
into the shades of saffron, amber, and green.

No children to carry you on, Helen.

Mine will strew my seed.
You will live on in this girl
catching her breath before lugging the hay
into the barn on your canvas
where a workhorse will nuzzle and nudge her
to feed him the last golden straws.

Crewel Work Bed Curtain

For M.K. Herbert, (English) 1692

Does M stand for Mary or Margaret?
Was she a Karen or Katherine, confined
to creating at home or in a convent
where women's art went unsung?

Her life story unfolds
in the leaves, buds and thorns of her rosebush
almost as tall as a tree embroidered
with wool and bulbous-eyed needles.

Chain Stitch, Back Stitch, Running Stitch
perfect for outlining branches.
Stem Stitch for stalks and vines,
Feather Stitch for finches
that scavenge rosehips for seeds.

Now "making its mark" at the Art Gallery*
I wonder what the curtain concealed.
Did it muffle her patron's nuptial night cries
or hide her thighs spread in childbirth?
Perhaps like Mademoiselle Boileau,
who always wore black,
the "sewing spinster" hired by my mother
and well-to-do friends in Quebec,
she plied her needle for clients
to dress them in Sunday silks.

Stitched roses, blooming through centuries of seasons,
laugh at snow, rain and drought.
Her tight-lipped sutures hold secrets,
guarded by firmly tied knots.

Olive-Ode

Shopping at Saint Lawrence Market
for a party tonight, I choose *Castelveltranos*
to serve with a crisp white wine
and the brine-cured, fruity *Cerignola*s
to complement a cheese tray.

Sampling a bitter *Tonda Iblea*,
I pinch out the pit and recall orchards in Sicily
with leathery lance-shaped leaves,
silver-grey undersides and fruit-laden branches
which symbolize peace
despite Saracen invasions.

I taste my bus trip through Agrigento
with my elderly mom twenty years ago.
Her *Valley of the Temples* memory
formed as a teen in ancient art-history class
hasn't been dulled by dementia.
But she now fails to filter out
her word-thistles and barbs as one does
olive oil from *Morescas* to reduce
its nuances of nettles.

Your skin is so coarse and pitted, I can see
every hole, even without glasses ...

I shrink as she glares
at my face instead of the olive grove
where tourists learn to handpick
without damaging
the plump, smooth-skinned *Verdellos*
and tiny black wrinkled *Minutas*
glistening like teardrops.

I Am Susanna Moodie

Moss Park, Toronto, Feb. 5, 2023
at the Metrolinx protest

I am here with you now at the park,
my bones barely holding together
after more than a century underground.

I lived my last years on your street, back then
just a muddy road a bit north of this park.
Though my brick house was strong,
I still worried about blizzards
and stray bears clawing my door.
I had recurrent nightmares
about my son, drowned in a creek years ago.

As for those trees we settlers chopped down
for ship masts and to beam
our first cabins near Lakefield,
why should I mourn them?
They were numerous.
Their hollows cradled our children
and coffined us when we died.

Enough for firewood forever
and paper for my journal-
guide to a bush settler's backbreaking life.
My books dispelled romantic notions
misleading Brits back home, who
dreamt of joining us here, for tea
taken from bone-china cups
before a hearth with a full bubbling
cauldron, in this land that feeds us
like royalty, even in brutal winter.

So, how did I learn the reason
why these trees were tied with yellow tape?

Well, as I once told my dear sister Catharine
when my toes began to tingle
as the sap was ready to run:
roots have their way of spreading news, you know.

Buried in my Belleville grave I heard rumours—
The culling was to make way for trains
that would rattle the slumbering residents
and tunnel into a future
made from steel and cement.

Today my rage kindles like birchbark
as I stand beside you in spirit,
witness to these giant oaks,
mere seedlings when I was a girl,
now felled, not by handsaw, nor axe,
but with cold, mechanical
arms and claws that level whole forests.

I once took pride in holding my tears,
but this thunder and thud as trunks topple,
preludes my weeping for our still green elders
whose ringed history they hold,
lopped, fallen, reduced
to sawdust and woodchips,
acorn hopes crushed.

233 Dundas Plaque

Susanna Moodie
(1803 to 1885) Chronicler of Life in Upper Canada
and Author of Roughing it in the Bush, lived at
233 Dundas Street East from 1881 to 1884.
Toronto Legacy Project and Heritage Toronto

Someone has defaced the plaque
where my last home stood.
They crossed out the four years I lived here,
blackened my name with paint.
As if that weren't enough, they took
sharp rocks to pock
the inscription written in block letters
on its royal blue background.

Surely it wasn't that half-naked
girl with pink and purple hair
dancing like a she-bear in heat?
She looks too caught up in fraught twirling
to bother with my history.

Even less likely, that boy cooking what looks like
lumpy white flour over a shivering flame.
He seems too sickly to have wielded
a weapon or paintbrush.

Could it be that stiffly coiffed woman wearing
a tailored suit with matching shoes and purse?
I doubt it … though she might consider me
"the sour cream of society" or "the fallen upper crust."

Genteel birth, officer husband, my privilege
did nothing to help us rise
above the stumps and uncouth Yankees in huts
north of Cobourg where I also
had to pluck chickens, sweep the dirt floor and bear
my children in a bed made from packing crates.

What's that cursing I hear?
It seems to come from some ruffians
cowled in corners behind
the pub near my home.
Lucky I'm just a spirit!
Their knives, no danger to me!

Gone are the days when we didn't lock our doors
and felt safe walking alone.

Muddy York, Hogtown, The Big Smoke …
My travels through time have shown me
Toronto the good and bad.
Now there's a chasm deeper than Lake Ontario
between the rich and poor.
People who can't afford rent
are harvested from the streets.

As for that shameless man
relieving himself on this tree …
To be fair, I can't blame him if he resents
my fenced property with beds
of fragrant pine needles
while he has to sleep on the cold sidewalk.

No Room Left

My Bubble

The Toronto Historic Distillery District

Flower boxes with sun-centered
orange pansies brighten the *Brewery* walls.

Waterfalls of white alyssum
with honey fragrance
adorn the *Old Mill* courtyard
as in a storybook romance.

My security bubble has cobblestone lanes
instead of a Yellow Brick Road.
It's also a dog-haven,
but no sign of Toto.

In my space-module,
a Christmas light constellation
strung above Trinity Lane
glows in the darkest months.
Luminous sculptures tint the snow
while well-heeled visitors
warmed with spirits and wine,
dine on lobster, Black Angus,
El Catrin's tasty tapas,
or *Cacao's* desserts.

In this, my safety-sphere,
plain-clothesmen keep watch.
Here in the Distillery District,
tents don't mushroom on sidewalks.
Nobody huddles in alcoves
or thaws themselves on vents.

My personal orb is translucent
as Chihuly's glass globes
that once graced the *Corkin Gallery*.
The man who fishes in dumpsters
doesn't dine at the *Oyster Bar*.
You won't meet the woman who carves her wrists
at the sculpture show.
The stranger prancing down Sackville,
who grabbed and squeezed me
so hard a rib cracked,
can't accost me.

I love my bubble,
home for twenty-five years.
But now I must move to a street
where the hard-hit will be my neighbours,
its membrane could burst.

Rehearsal

Moving from my spacious condo
into a "shoebox-flat",
I apologize to Dante, Shakespeare, Poe
and those friends whose books
I abandon at a second-hand store
in hopes they'll be re-homed.

Into a drop-off bin, I dump decades of clothing,
including my dead father's London Fog jacket,
mom's wedding dress, worn at my nuptials,
and three shopping bags
bulging with my ghost-dog's saved outfits.

Stopping at *Goodwill,* I cut the woolen umbilical
to my son's baby sweater, detach
myself from the frayed cord of the lamp
with two courtly figurines that were
waltzing in chipped ballroom gowns
even before I was born.

I gift my friend a fish-fossil,
then, under night's raincoat,
sneak my pebble collection
into a stranger's rock garden.

Bereft of most earthly goods
and left with a hand-tufted quilt
to cover my grief and guilt,
I dream this downsizing is just
a rehearsal for renouncing my skin-robe,
consigning my heart to burn
with the house of my bones.

Beautiful Poem

Today on my walk I'm ready to write
the most beautiful poem in the world.
I've been studying Wordsworth and am
on the lookout for imagery luminous as his
sun-steeped clouds and golden as his famous daffodils.

Half a block past my new home,
a rotting racoon lies buzzing beside a garbage bin
where an old man is foraging. I try to take in
the filigree rainbow of flies' wings,
but the stench makes me retch.
I turn a corner hoping my poem
might get musical, but the cacophony
of pile drivers, steam shovels, and cement mixers
raising yet another high-rise in this homeless city
shatters my harmony. When I reach Moss Park,
a man with crossed arms and closed eyes
sprawls across the cement walkway.
Should I call 911?

As I bend over him, he lets out a guttural snore.
I mutely shout: *You have the whole park to sleep in,
why are you lying here, spoiling my poem?*

Further on, a dozen tents the colour of mouldy
mushrooms sprout from the grass
while a youth pisses on a rosebush.
Speechless, my poem turns its back on me.
I kill the draft then write down raw impressions.
This piece becomes a prose-poem fighting for its life.

Elsewhere

Today on the streetcar a man spews
obscenities and flings felafel balls
and handfuls of salad at us riders.

Wiping hummus from my hair,
I'm angry enough to wish
people like him could be rocketed
into outer space
to perish on airless planets,
so, when I'm asked
where the new shelters should be
for those with no roof but the sky
my only answer is:
build those damn shelters elsewhere—
until I cool off and admit
that I might need refuge someday
if I forget my address
or a sinkhole opens in my brain.

Barely Afloat

October 15th, downtown Toronto.
Palms reach out in front of grocery stores,
restaurants, and shops.
A young man eyeballs my purse then corners me.
Caught in the 5 pm tide, I feel like a fish without fins:
a suckerfish.

I offer a granola bar
but he shakes a fist in my face and growls,
Don't want that. Five bucks for a sandwich.
Make it a tenner.

If I refuse, will he follow me?
To get rid of him, I fork over
a fiver he sure as hell won't use for food.
Casually well-dressed, clearly well-fed,
obviously trolling for drug-dollars,
perhaps an overdose will kill him.

What's happening to me? I used to be kind.
When my dad took me fishing, I fed
the fish bread instead of baiting my hook.

Still there are some I'm compelled to help stay afloat:
the friendly old woman
housed beneath an umbrella,
the man with leaking sores
and plastic bags for shoes.

As for that grasping menace
who made my hands tremble,
I'd like to chop his off.

No Nurse Nightingale

Outside the Daisy Mart
where I stop to buy milk
a ragged old man pulls down his pants.
A catheter tube plugged into his penis,
he cradles his bag of urine
the colour of amber rum.

I sneak my shadow past him
then hotfoot it down my street
to hide in my gated community
where sparrows sing in bare bushes
and I dream of flying to Florida
to bask on a smooth beach
under a floral umbrella
as I sip pineapple pina colada
and lose myself in a novel.

Good Neighbour Poem

11 p.m., Toronto,
two nights before Victoria Day
POP POP POP   POP POP POP
a volley of six shots
in the backyard adjoining mine.

I lie in bed petrified,
blinds pulled down,
waiting for screams or sirens to sound, worried

about my drug-dealing "neighbours"
who shred my sleep fighting and fucking
in their dogshit and garbage-strewn concrete yard.

Do blood roses explode from bullet wounds,
or were they just sky-scaping
with early fireworks?

My dreams vaporized,
I don't call the police.
A murderous wish
black as the moon's dark side
eclipses my once sunny soul.

Hooked

Coming home from *the Golden Diner*, I discover
a young man with long matted hair
and a blissed-out air, sitting in the alcove
in front of my gated complex.
His back braced by a brick wall,
legs stretched across the entrance,
he sucks on a glass pipe.

Snowflakes land like moths
on his loose-knit sweater; I worry
he might perish in this sub-zero weather.

Should I invite him into the foyer?
Give him a warm corner
to come down from his high?
Leave him enough money to buy a burger
and fries when he wakes up ravenous?

Should I call the police?
Or, perhaps safer for him: the Salvation Army.

Knowing he might never clasp a hand reaching out,
should I just ignore him?

As I tiptoe over his legs, the man remains
in a haze that smells like a chemical fire.

The door springs shut behind me.
I recall my own adult son
still recovering from addiction
and writhe on the hook
of my sleep-robbing questions.

No Room Left

A senryu sequence

fiery maple leaves
burn to a frostbitten crisp
homeless shadows drift
  *

with no address he
unpacks his cardboard suitcase
all over the street
  *

I hold out five bucks
to a tattered man. A faster
hand snatches it
  *

green traffic light. I wait
for the guy on the far side
to zip up his fly
  *

in Moss Park gardens
a tall girl sleeps in a bed
of bent sunflowers
  *

sparrows feast on seeds
food trucks arrive every day,
feed those without wings
  *

rising breath, cold clouds
shivering people line up
for open shelters
  *

street cleaners arrive,
sweep away last night's garbage
four frozen bodies

Until

After a pen and ink drawing by T.G. Hamilton

The artist shows me his drawing
of the Irish in Black '47
surfacing from a *coffin ship.*
My untapped tears overflow.

Victims of typhus and famine
sown by colonial greed,
skin-rags hang from their skeletons,
oozing eyes with homesick looks
scan the strange new land.

Do I weep for my ancestral kin
because my tears feel safe?

I don't have to carry the sick from the docks,
anoint their sores in the fever sheds
or clean up their vomit and shit
as did those nuns who risked
their lives to save the stricken.

My tears glint like the gems
in my mother's heirloom brooch
I won't have to pawn
to buy them food and ointment.

As for the people on my city streets,
who barely breathe on subway vents,
or curl up in door-wells,

until I'm willing to do more than weep with them,
my teardrops will be useless as broken glass.

Young Man Lying in a Church Doorwell

He is as beautiful as Michelangelo's David
taking a break from his pedestal,
to nap near the cathedral entrance
guarded by stone gargoyles.

Awed by his fine-chiselled features,
muscular form and smooth brow,
my tears well up as I notice blueberry bruises
with punctured stars at their centres
constellating his bare arms,
and the empty gold-labeled bottle
telltale on the cement.

I picture him in ten years:
his classical nose broken,
silky skin coarse as burlap,
perfect teeth gone to brown stubs,
and the saddest scenario—
his flesh, cold as marble.

Recalling the nightmare craving
that gnawed my own son's guts,
and my sleepless nights
tied to my umbilical phone cord
as he battled his Goliath …

I'm no believer in miracles
or a Divine Father watching over his children,
yet I'm tempted to enter this nave and light
whole tiers of candles to celebrate
my son's five sober years,
and offer a prayer for this youth
as if I were his mother too.

Danse Macabre

Waiting for the 8 pm bus at the corner
of Sherbourne and Shuter, I spot
a man in a funereal coat.
His face shrouded in a scarf,
arms like injured wings,
he teeters in the middle of the street,
flapping before oncoming traffic.

Is he addicted to four-wheel roulette?
Trying to off himself?
Fund his next fix?
Is he the guy my neighbour described?
Any moment now, he's roadkill.

My legs shake.
What can I do?
The lights change.
Cars miss him by inches.

I don't pretend he is none of my business
or slink away into the night.

Yesterday I bypassed a man holding a "hungry" sign,
averted my eyes from someone's lost granny,
and ignored a feral teen the same age as my grandson.

Tonight, I loot my purse.
Braving the traffic
to draw that man back onto the sidewalk,
I wave a twenty in his face.
He grabs it like a green flag
and lurches into the darkness.

Sidestepping

A pantoum

Scared of jogging in Moss Park
full of tents and punctured people
I get high on country music
when I dance in my living room

Full of tents and punctured people
bodies blocking park paths
I dance in my living room
sidestepping syringes and needles

Bodies blocking park paths
I cha-cha, boogie and shuffle
sidestepping syringes and needles
I play country music full blast

Cha-cha, boogie and shuffle
pop tunes and hurtin' songs
I play country music full blast
my routine timed with a stopwatch

Pop tunes and hurtin' songs
I'm high on country music
my routine timed with a stopwatch
scared of jogging in Moss Park

First Snow, Toronto 2024

White firmament fallen
on roofs and lawns,
courtyard maples sparkle,
dormant rosebushes gleam.

Brushing glitter from my down coat,
last night's news flickers
across my mind. I shiver
for those sunburnt countries
where ash that precipitates
from both sides of the sky
isn't a weather event.

Flakes from exploded cities
settle on skins of survivors
fleeing toward *safe zones*
soon to be stormed
by the next unnatural blizzard
shrouding their homes and hearts.

Drone as Jewelry

Instead of predator-planes, imagine
micro drones with gold filigree wings,
sapphire and ruby eyes,
brooches perched on lapels
instead of landing pads.

Rather than cowering in bomb shelters
or under basement beams,
picture people admiring
each other's droneflies pinned
to dresses, saris and burkas,
fedoras, turbans and tuques.

In lieu of purple hearts,
bronze crosses and medals,
these mini drone-badges might adorn
the uniforms of those who refuse
to launch ballistic missiles.

Instead of spitfire words
and whistling shells
we daily aim at each other,
imagine ourselves as jewelers
whose gems wing their way
to land on the laps of children
who will only ever learn
from their parents to fold
paper airplanes.

Whirlybirds

For Dai

Orange helicopters shadow
my Toronto courtyard several times a day.

Chack-chack-chak-a-chak-chak
their staccato rotor-blade-rhythms
drown out our resident robin,
and woodpecker's *rat-a-tat-tat*.

No aptitude for nest-building or egg-warming,
these whirlybirds rescue children,
airlift burn victims
and carry women in labour in their bellies,
all whose life hangs by a beat.
Bypassing traffic jams, they skirt
wingless construction cranes.

As one hovers over
Saint Michael's Hospital rooftop helipad,
my bed frame and porch rail vibrate,
the springs of my soul shake.
Accursed metal bird!
Loud as the jackhammer breaking up concrete!

My friend's husband flew
in a search and rescue *Sea King* for years.
Sometimes flashbacks of the people
he couldn't save chop up his sleep.
Grateful he rescued so many,
I hear the sky whirling again
and bless these incoming birds.

Birdshot

The *Globe and Mail* lands
on my doorstep with a thump.
On the front page a young woman
with long, uncovered hair
wears an eyepatch.

In photos on page 8, other protestors
blinded by guns loaded with birdshot
show off "badges of honour"
after the Islamic Revolutionary Guard
exploded their retinas
and they wept tears of blood.

Sparrows perch on my balcony railing.
I break peanuts into pieces
the size of birdshot.
Watching them feed and fight, I'm awed
by that brave Kurdish woman who flew
in the face of a guard
and later posted to the world:
You aimed at my eyes, but my heart is still beating.

The name of the woman pictured on the front page of
the *Globe and Mail*, January 12, 2024, is Mersedeh
Shahinkar. The quotation was posted on Instagram by
another woman blinded by Iranian government forces,
Elaheh Tavakolian.

In the Forest of the Night

After "The Tyger" by William Blake
Mariupol, March 9, 2022

Here in Canada, my grandson will be born
in a hospital. He will be placed
at his mother's breast to taste sweet life.
Later, swaddled in a flannel blanket,
he will sleep in a crib built from beechwood.

Family and friends will come
bearing gifts; some giving
thanks to their god.

Tempted to fold my hands
and fall on my knees,
I will do neither.

Holding my new grandson, I will recall
the news from another forested country
where snow shrouds
pine needles and bare branches
of aspen, birch and maple.
There, a mother with a mounded belly
pleads for her baby's life as she bleeds
on a stretcher rushed from a bombed hospital.

That night, they both die.

My Lord, I will question
if you exist, by *what art*
do you watch over one birth,
yet turn your back on another?

If I Were a House

The Puppy

Shawinigan Falls, 1947

Me and my friend Ann are five.
Her Uncle Max is minding us
'cuz her mum and dad are at the hospital
waiting for the stork.

It's dark and snowing stars.
The river is a long white scarf.

My Red-River coat, woolen leggings
and mittens are warm enough for tobogganing.
Ann wraps her legs around Uncle Max,
and I wrap mine around Ann.
Whee! We whizz to the bottom of the hill.
No streetlamps here. No houses or people.

Come closer, darlings, so you can see the puppy
who sleeps in my pocket, Uncle Max whispers.
Come closer and keep him warm.
The pup's just been fed by his mom
and might spit up some milk.

Puppy! I've never seen one before,
though I sometimes pet the black dog
who lives near the grocery store.
I can hardly wait as Uncle Max opens his pocket.

Eww, how come he doesn't have legs? Ann asks.
Sausage dog, not fully grown, Max grins.
Now stroke him real nice and watch him stand up.
Good Girl, Good Girl! Your turn now, Donna.

Uncle Max's breath, hot in my face.
I hate the look of his puppy

with only one eye and no tail,
but I take off my mittens and do what I'm told
'cuz he's Ann's uncle.

Uncle Max's hand around mine, we pump
the pup till he burps up warm milk.
I am a good girl too.

Next afternoon, stork still hasn't come.
Be good and listen to Uncle Max,
Ann's dad shakes a finger at us
as he leaves for the hospital again.

Ginger ale and chocolate chip cookies.
A party under the stairwell.
We do everything Uncle Max wants
'cuz we're scared Ann's father will spank
her bare bum and stop us playing together.

Back home, I wash my sticky fingers.
Again and again. Pink sausage dog. Milk. Spit up.
I throw up chocolate chip eyes in the toilet.

You haven't even touched your fries, Mom says.
I tell her about the puppy.
Her eyes get round and mad.
She hugs me then calls Ann's dad on the party line.
A week later, Uncle Max is in jail.
She says he'll never come near us again.
Me and Ann dig a pit in a snowbank.
We pretend Uncle Max is inside.
We feed him frozen dog poo.
I can't eat my own dinner all winter.

Revisiting the House on Hart Street
Shawinigan Falls, 2016

That heron-legged girl loved
to sketch horses with charcoal,
shoot her siblings with her daisy cap gun,
ring neighbours' doorbells then leap
behind a snowbank to hide.

That six-year-old girl almost stopped
breathing forever because of her Persian cat.
She imagined God owned a gift shop,
a heaven store full of free
McIntosh toffee, gumdrops, and ginger ale.

Sixty years later I revisit the red brick house
with the *hat-roof* pulled over its eyes
where she lived with her razor-tongued
mother, sphinx father, and two bratty brothers
who tore at each other like the fighting cocks
her Irish Grandmother once raised.

I shed that girl when she grew too old to wear
winged Maple seeds on her nose,
bury herself in piled leaves,
or play "doctor" with a friend under the porch.

Today's doctors treat my sore spine and knees
that bother me as I walk by number nine Hart Street.
Just then a girl flies out the front door
with a polite "Bonjour Madame."

I house these memories,
and the place I remember is home to a child.

Barron Lake, Summer 1953

The rented ramshackle farmhouse
with a privy but no running water on our first holiday.
Mom sweats as she primes the stiff-armed
pump in the weedy front yard.
Ashes powdering her face, she scrubs
the cast-iron stove and lugs in firewood
while mosquitoes raise red welts on her arms.

I wheeze through the nights in my mouldy room.
She plasters my chest with *Vicks VapoRub*
and cradles me in my bed.

Mom's blue eyes, dark-ringed as a racoon's,
she boils baby Brian's diapers,
rinses them from the rowboat.

Two merciless weeks of rain—
she helps me sew tiny birchbark canoes,
plays Go Fish with Gary and Greg,
roasts marshmallows over the stove with us
and reads aloud from the adventures of Goofy
vacationing in *Gruesome Gulch*.

Seven decades later, brother Gary and I
revisit Barron Lake where mom showed us
how to *dog paddle* with our front paws,
and float on our backs like otters
soaking themselves in the sky.

Having spent years caring for my mother—
gravy-stained clothes I cleaned,
insults I bore while avoiding her hickory cane
through her descent into dementia.
Gazing across sunlit water,
I now release gathered grudges,
so many stones I'm skipping.

Handmaidens, 1955

My grade-four teacher, Sister Celine
hands us girls mimeographed copies
of chasubles, stoles and maniples
worn by the priest at mass.
We crayon them in liturgical colours—
violet, green, red, white and gold
while altar boys learn to swing incense,
tinkle the Sanctus bells,
shape their lips around Latin
and hold the paten under the chins
of communicants who tongue up the wafers.

The kitchen-nuns roll, slice and bake
in the woodstove that wilts their wimples,
smoke-stains their skins,
while their sisters, the laundry-nuns
sweating in coarse woolen habits,
handwash, starch and iron
the lace-trimmed surplices
sewn by the ones who thread
their paths to the Lord one stitch at a time
and pray with pins in their mouths.

The tenth child of a French farmer
given away to the church
for the price of a small dowry*
to secure his own spot in heaven,
middle-aged Sister Celine,
who once dreamed of bearing her own child,
calls us schoolgirls her *daughters*.
She unlocks a storage cupboard,
takes out the creche for us.

Her expectations during Advent
about to be fulfilled,
she joins the joists of the stable,
buffs the tarnished star.

Grooming the plaster donkey,
she places it near the manger
filled with immaculate straw,
rounds up the sheep stored in egg-cartons
to graze on a green cloth meadow.

She dusts Mary, Joseph and the three Kings,
placing each figurine.

The peak of her labour at hand,
my favourite handmaiden struggles
to free the Christ Child
swaddled in last year's newsprint
and tied in a paper bag 'womb.'

She cuts the purple cord,
cradles Him in her palms,
his head
          his shoulders
                    sweet body
delivered at last to the world.

Turning the Pages

In her eighties,
mom scaled Mount Everest,
leaning into the slope,
thigh muscles burning
while the sunrise set the sky on fire.

On Brazil's Rio Negro, she watched
snakes pop up periscope-heads,
kids swim with piranhas.
A bite from a Paraponera ant
laid her up for a week.

In her nineties, she floated
above Masai Mara's plains
marveling at giraffes and elephants
and the wild-fire sunset
as she sipped tea
in a hot air balloon basket.

Nearing her journey's end,
she charted the heavens
with Teilhard de Chardin,
orbited with Sally Ride,
flew her last chapter
in a nursing home wheelchair.

Now that I too have turned
eight decades of pages,
I take mom's books from my shelf
and travel with her in my rocker
to those very same places.

Non-Combustible

My brother jokes
that I look ready for the grave,
brings in two logs
and a handful of kindling.

As he stokes the fire, I fume
and fold his unread newspaper
into a dunce cap
imagining it on his ash-white head
until the flames consume him
and my rage is quenched.

He comes back, almost eighty,
not as the taunting dark-haired teen
I wanted to kill when he nicknamed
my boyfriend "The Lobster"
nor the middle-aged debt collector
with his coal-black humour,
but as he is today: my warm-hearted brother
a mere two years younger,
who bakes cookies for me,
treats me to shows at the Legion
and laughs when his dog licks me
as we hike the old railway line.

Bones, brittle as chalk,
body, held together
by strawberry stitches from failed surgeries,
maybe his inflammatory jest
just means
infirmity craves company.

Maid

This maid is no floor-scrubbing servant
girl who washes clothes in a river.

She's no handmaid of the Lord,
virgin who opened her soul
instead of her legs to conceive.

Neither is she mermaid, bridesmaid, Old Maid,
nor *Maid of the Mist* crossing
Niagara's white-water border
for a breath-taking view of the Falls.

This is the acronym I contemplate while
trembling in the oral surgeon's chair—

M.A.I.D could end my jaw pain forever,
stop my lopsided tongue
from lolling and garbling my words
should the lump prove malignant.

Back in eighty-seven
my mother-in-law had no recourse to this MAID.
The surgeon pulled her rotting teeth, and cut
her tumorous tongue, leaving only a stub.

I pray I won't have to enlist her.

Even after I'm spared
rejoicing that my lump is benign,
MAID, Lady in Waiting
needling my dreams,
embroiders a long red silk scarf.

For the Doctor on Ward B

I condemn you to rot in the hospital bed
you implied my dear friend was malingering in,
two days after the speeding car struck him
in the middle of a crosswalk with a lit-up pedestrian sign.
His pelvis, quadruple-fractured,
he can no longer walk, stand, or even sit.

Yes, you dared suggest if only he had the willpower
he would rise from this bed, leaving it vacant
for someone in the packed waiting room
supposedly worse off than him.

Or maybe consumed by greed
you were so set on getting a raise and praise
for a lightning turnover of beds
you forgot it was your job to know
my friend could barely shift an inch.

I sentence you to fester for months in that bed
where you'd have to pee like he did
in a cardboard container that leaked
all over his overbed table.

Your torture time would include
twenty-three hours without eating
a morsel or drinking a drop while you awaited
surgery that no one comes to tell you
has been bumped to another day.

Your white-coated tongue,
voice too hoarse to cry out,
your hell would include a visit
from some inhuman prick like yourself.

Songster

His warm tenor lilts
through sterile rooms and corridors.
Even get-well bouquets on the windowsills
lift their drooping heads.
The lumbering laundry and meal cart procession
rumbles to a halt as everyone lingers to listen
to the rhythmic *Tennessee Waltz*.

Ten days after being hit by the car
that fractured his pelvis
leaving him unable to move,
our mutual friend texts me: *Good news!*
Tom is in an armchair, singing fortissimo!

I picture the nurses smiling,
doctors pausing on their rounds,
bed-ridden patients, sick of
the clicks and beeps of monitors,
humming along.

Is this just the morphine singing?

I know song is as natural to Tom as to a bird
and remember him crooning in my kitchen
as he dipped bread into egg batter
for our golden French toast.

Itinerant maestro, he intoned
at nuptials and in nursing' homes
where he cheered folks with *Hey Good Lookin'*
and helped their souls escape
on the wings of *I'll Fly Away*.

He whistled with the cardinals in my courtyard,
trilled with a Cedar Waxwing
and mimicked melodious robins.

I'm convinced that when
his morphine drip stops,
euphoria's rainbow fades
and that car flashes back
as he struggles to stand on his own,
my brave friend, in love
with life's *belle canto* range
will never stop being a songster
in both heavens and hells of this world.

Tom Swimming

I love to watch you swimming in Lake Ontario.

At home with the "lakers" and "salties,"
wind-surfers with handheld sails,
the sunken ships and planes,
ashes of some of our friends,
you float and bob near the buoys.
Above you, lines of gulls
ripple and undulate like the ones
in Rachmaninoff's "Sea and Seagulls"
that flew from your violin.

Your arms stroking our "inland sea,"
feet kicking up diamonds,
you front crawl towards the breakwater
where three brown and white cygnets
are dabbling for aquatic plants.

As I lounge in a blue beach chair
minding your sunhat and mandolin,
looking forward to your serenades,
and new poem you'll swan from the depths,
I soar with a dragon kite
and watch two wet dogs
waiting for the next stick to fly,
but what I love most is this:

After your fill of the lake,
you will wave, then swim towards me.

Instead of a forgotten towel,
I will hold out my arms.

Astrid's Ark

England hasn't seen the sun for weeks.
I'm going to build us an ark, quips my elderly cousin
with sea-green eyes and a rainproof smile.
I shiver under a blanket
while my clothes steam on the rads.

Built from her stories, their beams and ballast,
Astrid's ark will house her Irish grandpa's
two white stallions with blanched plumes for weddings
and a pair of midnight mares wearing
coal-black feathers for funerals.
The great vessel will welcome her six siblings,
three daughters and cousin Gerard
with his 37 Friesian cows
and the bottle-fed calf known as "142"
who grew up tilting her chin for a scratch
in the milking parlour.

There'll be a berth for the red fox she found
sunning himself on the roof of a car,
a corner for "Cookie" her cat,
but not for the rats Astrid used to trap live
and release in faraway fields.

As for the ark's captain, she asserts,
I learned to sail in my teens
then bought my own boat
after my marriage floundered.
I discovered where the reefs are
and how to avoid them.

Now I navigate by tapping
this white cane on the sidewalk,
not expecting to see rainbows in colour,

though I do reach for a grey olive branch
such as the one I offered my father,
who worked so hard on the farm,
he never had time for his children.
As for those parasite priests who fawned
over Mother, wallowing in her hospitality,
and weaseling stipends for masses,
after hearing that some had abused children,
I imagined them drowning.

The deluge persists.
The heavens pour forth as I recall
Astrid and I were born the same year
under Fall's star-skeined sky.

My hair, salt-white and flowing,
my skin, barnacled,
I take my place on her ark
borne toward the unknown.
Sipping hot rum from a mug,
I trade a few tales of my own
about those who sank me, and others,
like Astrid, who keep me afloat.

Closet Nocturne

Midnight, I unzip
myself from head to toe
and step out of my skin.

Naked and free, I open
my closet. Run my fingers over
the skins of my past swinging
on bone hangers.

My rose-petal smooth
little girl skin
barely comes up to my navel, now.

My teenage pelt, slathered in zit-cream,
chides me for insisting
that age doesn't matter.

I try on my middle-aged
neatly pressed and preserved
school-teacher hide.
The starched fabric chafes.

Sloughing it off,
I wake still wearing
my well-worn comfy skin.
These pouches, pockets,
furrows and folds
will cover my bones to the end
just like the closest of friends.

If I were reborn as a poem

I'd come back as an ode
that celebrates the ordinary—

mother making rice pudding
with raisins and cinnamon,
my sweetheart filling the feeders
for hummingbirds with wingspans
the width of his mustache,
my grandson plays
with my glow-in-the-dark
wristwatch greening his hand.

An ode that brims over with wonder,
applauds marble Venus de Milo
and the flaws of my misaligned spine.

An ode that crosses the border
to a body of water,
dark, yet with a sheen.

Unlike haiku or sonnet's tight cage,
my ode would roam the savannah,
free as a gazelle.

Let me live on
as a book of odes
passed hand to hand.

My readers might open the covers
inviting as chapel doors.

After Reading Nobel Prize Winning Poets

Sometimes my mind is a green budgie
jealous of a cardinal's red plumage,
a peacock's fan with formidable eyes
and a magpie's smart script tracked in sand.
Yes, I want to pull out bird-of-paradise pinions,
peck holes in a Quetzal's eggs
and murder their hatchling poems.

Neighbours

In the courtyard of my new urban home
a House Wren reclaims her old nest
in the hollow of a bent Silver Birch
with black sentinel eyes.

Placing twigs,
plumping dry grass and cobwebs
lining her egg basket
built far from cat and racoon reach,
she warns them with whirring churrs.

I guard my nest:
row house with guest room and fireplace.
Tome-laden bookshelves bar my back door.
I change my front door lock,
install a glass orb-webcam.

But the best alarm
heard each morning
through my open window
is the House Wren's burbling.

His Eye Is on the Sparrow

Matthew 6:25-27

At the porch feeder,
my eyes prefer the cardinal,
his fiery crest,
pulpit voice and playboy whistle.

When his mate appears
flashing green in white snow feathers
drifting from January clouds, I'm breathless.

I'm courting a bluejay,
not with flowers and candy
but with almonds.
I woo chickadees puffy as whole notes,
but have no eyes for brown sparrows.

Nonetheless their flock
swoops down, flapping,
chirp-chirping.
They hail me as the goddess
blessing their bellies with breadcrumbs,
unsalted peanuts and seeds.

In my ashen coat
I pen this plainsong.
Pray, who am I to shun them?

I beseech the Sky Lord
that his eye might favour me too.

If I Were a House

For André

I'd be my son's cottage on Georgian Bay.

I would stand tall and stark
in my painted white coat
shadowed by creamy birches
and the creaking masts of poplars
with leafy wind-frayed sails.

Shoulder to shoulder with mammoth
Precambrian boulders, I'd hear
the waves carving my shoreline,
eating away the archipelago
made by a mythical giant
who dropped a mountain that shattered.

In summer, I'd welcome hummers
to the red plastic petunias my son hung
from my balcony and I'd watch
a hawk sizing up jays gorging
on suet and corn while a Red Fox waits
to pounce on a chipmunk stealing
the spilled kernels.

When my son drives up here from his city life
to replenish his feeders
and spend a weekend with me,
I'd listen for
the crunch of his footsteps
on the gneiss-pebbled path.
My blue door would throw itself open,
all my windows light up.

Enough

For René

My dear son,
isn't it enough that I'm glad
you're now living in your dream
lakeside cottage on a fringe of forest.
You wake to woodsmoke fragrance
from your potbelly stove, delight
in deer grazing on corn, bran and beechnuts
you scattered under the pines
adorned with snow cones and crystals.

Isn't it enough for me to know, after
your acrid divorce and loss of your
children whose coldness caverns your heart,
you are happily remarried. New friends
welcome you to their hearths and ice fishing huts
to share hot chocolate and brandy.

Isn't it more than enough
that a few years ago a surgeon planted
two stents in your arteries
so blood flows like sap through spiles
in your tapped sugar maples.
You can now run, walk your dogs and play hockey
without struggling for breath.

Today you journey from your haven
where the moon lanterns the lake.
You drive through Precambrian Shield,
brave a ghost-highway, and crawl through
whiteout to reach us, your kin.

It is enough to brim my own crater
as we talk at this Yuletide table.
I hold you close as when you were a child,
neither of us ever dreaming then
that my own marriage would break
like a bough in a snowstorm,
I would leave you to live in my own wilderness.

Ode to Park Benches

Blessed be park benches,
their backs bracing ours.

They wear fiery shawls in Fall,
white scarves in Winter, and the cracked
caps of Spring's tree-bud sheathes.

In Summer swelter, walkers rush to them like water,
while their dogs shelter beneath.
In Sonora Park desert, I asked my sweetheart
How far from this bench to the next one
as if they were signposts to the heavenly chill
of our airconditioned car.

Yes, glory be benches made from wood,
recycled plastic, wrought iron, stone and concrete.
Praise be their nails, nuts and bolts,
the machine-made and hand-crafted.
Carved with forest sprites, bless
those gouged with graffiti
and the rainbow-hued semi-circular ones
that can seat a crowd.

On my way home from Saint Lawrence Market
laden with grocery bags, I head for a row of
green benches bearing memorial brass plates.

If benches could gossip imagine
the stories they'd share about those
who laughed, wept, or slept on the slats,
aired their secrets and crimes,

drank coffee, communed with a bottle,
settled to feed pigeons, read, write, or daydream.

How well they serve us as confessionals,
beds for those with newspaper pillows,
a resting place for Basho's ghost,
pews in a forest cathedral.

Homesick in Miami

No fishing
No boating
No swimming
No unaccompanied children
No pets
Beware of alligators
Please do not feed
or provoke—I heed

the warning signs
in front of the turquoise ponds
scalloped and groomed
to manmade perfection
while I pine for

a glacier-carved
northern Ontario lake where I might
spot a loon guarding
her nest in the reeds
fish for muskies and bass
canoe to my heart's content
skinny dip at dusk
and best of all, there are

no alligators sunbathing
on my favourite Precambrian boulder
or lurking like logs with eyes
to snack on one of my grandkids
or swallow my small dog

What I Love About You

For Jim

Elephants can hear
low frequency noises 4 km away

Bats use high-pitched echolocation
perfect for navigating darkness

Birds listen for distant storms
to begin migration

Baleen and Fin Whales employ sound waves
for long range reception

Tigers attract mates with infrasound
while crocodiles head-slap the water

I, myself wear hearing aids
but often lose a connection

yet you, my love without wings, fins, antennae
or manmade aids, can hear in a heartbeat

what I need, even when I am silent,
or thousands of miles away.

Hark!

Birthday Dream

After John Oughton's "Tunnel In"

The only instruction is that you fill in the blank form then follow your umbilical cord back to the tunnel where you arrive naked. A warm day is advisable. Do not wear fur, feathers or leaves on your hairless head. If you need a guide, your mother is here. She will remember herself howling, waking the world when you crowned. She will claim your body was blue then your first breath turned it red. Follow the thread back through the tunnel, careful not to get hit by a train. Ride the escalator up to the sunrise then grow a longer umbilical. Follow its length all your life so you can be daily reborn.

Ode to Elation

A take-off on "Sorrow" by Shara McCallum

There are not enough odes to elation.
Why not add one more to its hot air balloon basket?

Once upon a take-off invites a windfall. We forget
mid-flight the wax wings of elation.

I stay awake nightly rehearsing my lift-off.
Tomorrow I'll air my affair with elation.

A surgeon is cutting a kite string. Who cares?
I blow bubbles of elation.

We're given a choice to lift ourselves up
or to pinprick our own elation.

Buttercups, birth of my grandson,
baptismal bells of elation.

I shout his name to the sky
It spells it out in contrails. Elation

Elation
Elation!

Hark!

My surname is King.
If I'd been one of the Magi,
I'd have set out in the dark—
but instead of a camel
through the desert and mountains,
I'd ride the 501 Queen streetcar
to Saint Michael's hospital
where I'd wait for the slow elevator
crowded with strangers.
   Hark! I wouldn't bring
gold, myrrh, or frankincense,
I'd forget my wallet and coat,
and just bring my half-naked self
awakened by the good news.
I'd get off at the fifth floor,
race the wrong way down the hall
till a nurse shepherded me.
   I'd fly though the open door
of the maternity ward where
hark! Instead of the Christ-child
my grandson, long-limbed and strong
lay swaddled in a blue cotton blanket,
asleep in a straw-less plastic manger.
   Holding him now, for the first time,
I forget about the star shining on the stable,
oxen, sheep and three kings, knowing
I'd give anything to be his saviour.

Six Hours Old
(Grandson)

Getting to know me,
mother traces
the roundness of my reddish face,
fluffs up the down on my head,
her fingertip light as a leaf.

She strokes my puffy eyelids,
brushes the bridge of my nose,
follows my spinal ridge
to fondle each bluish toe, while you

without a mother to caress you this way
for more decades than my little hours,
relive her long-ago touch,
your skin tingling with bliss.

April

(Grandson)

I arrived on April Fools' Day,
my cord wrapped round my neck.
Even so, I was born smiling
and slipped through that noose
like the rain that slid through
the downspout on the hospital roof.

By August I laughed
at everything—
a ball bouncing past my nose,
my teddy bear flying,
a banana that fell to the floor.
Tears were never my treasure,
the world, a court to amuse me.

But you, who were born late September
when Fall severs its stems,
remember my dark umbilical,
and are slow to join in my laughter.

Explorer

As a child, oblivious
to what curiosity might come to kill,
I was curious about new world explorers,
themselves driven by curiosity
about the world which was always new.

Today in their footsteps and mine
my two-month-old grandson, Leo
is discovering
the continent of his belly,
gulfstream in his diaper,
saltwater tears,
peninsula fingers
and the silk road between his mouth
and his mother's breasts.

Thirsting for more than milk,
lacking, as yet, the spyglass, lantern, canoe,
saddle horse and logbook of language,
soon he will crawl, walk and run
across life's landscape,
guided by his compass—
curiosity.

Killing the Fly

My son James, the ballet school pianist
whose fingers dance on keyboards,
        now pirouettes around the kitchen
whapping walls with a dishtowel
            to kill a crazed fly.
Leo, my eight-month-old grandson,
roars with delight.

To enhance this revelry, I grab
a towel as well. Doing *glisses*
and *jetes* like the ballerinas my son plays for,
        I thwack the cupboards,
            fridge and stove.

James whacks the floor and door
while Leo, now red-faced with glee,
pounds his highchair tray.

Looking back on our comedy's
choreographed slapstick
and our lopsided laughter—
are we teaching him that killing is fun?

Is the sequel to this smacking spree
the snap and flip of a mouse trap,
a boxing ring *pas de deux*,
or the hanged man's jig?

Baby Neptune

For my grandson, Leo

Your umbilicus was cut 15 months ago.
Now an invisible cable still runs
to the mothership.

When she, sea-goddess with brimming breasts,
needs to leave harbour for a few
office-hours while I babysit,
you storm her departure.

Clinging to her leg like a mast,
you rage and howl,
assail her with a typhoon of tears.

I've had my own tantrums,
so I can relate, Baby Neptune.
I still seethe beneath my smooth surface
when I feel abandoned.

You won't let me sooth or comfort you yet,
but I can wait.

The very image of your tempestuous father,
to some degree still moored to me,
you too will soon learn
how to live bound to your mom,
even as you set sail.

Alphabet Rug

On my grandson's playroom floor
lies the rubber alphabet rug.
The letters are inserted
into interlocking squares.

He crawls to the capital "I",
yanks it free.

Why always "I", never any other letter?

He gums the stem,
gnaws on that synthetic bone,
flings it across the room,
and fetches it like a dog.

I flash back to my own
tall, thin ego, that I've raised
up, only to knock down.
I've turned it into an icicle
to freeze out would-be friends,
blamed myself for flunking two marriages
and beat myself with its rod.

In life's playroom, where "I"
can be bent into a question mark,
my answer is all the good things I've been—

Cook, camp councillor, teacher, poet
and grandma who gave up her house
so her grandson could have room to play,
I get an "A" from the alphabet rug
and hug it to my chest.

Watch

Leo is licking my wristwatch,
trying out his baby teeth.

Stretching the elastic strap, he tries
to insert his toes, fingers, then nose.

Master of small disasters,
will he set my life backwards, forwards
or stop time altogether
by jamming its wheels and cogs
or feeding my watch to Abby,
the dog he thinks is his?

Tonight, my timepiece is his plaything
while I, whom Time has dressed
in skin rags and toyed with my ticker,
retrieve my watch in return for a cookie,
glad that the little thief
knows nothing yet
about expiring batteries.

Full Circle

At eighteen months, my grandson
can't tell time, but at 5 o'clock sharp
he listens for the turn of the front door key
and his father's soft-soled footsteps.

Abandoning his matchbox cars,
favourite toy piano
and Big Bird on Sesame Street,
he runs down the hall
like a bear cub to honey.

My son, who grew up without a father,
scoops up his toddler and laughs:
How's my Prince Pepito?
As he imitates a trumpet's bright tones
playing a royal fanfare, I recall
forty years ago, when I came back from teaching
my son toddled into the daycare room
and stretched out his arms to me.

His silky cheek pressed against
my powdered one,
sticky hands in my hair
milky breath mingling with mine,
I still see the purple circle
my lipstick left on his forehead
as I called him "my little King."

Gift

In star-speckled pyjamas,
         Leo leaps
                    into my lap,
wraps his arms around me,
gives me a good night kiss.

Back in my bed,
I'll skip the typical soporifics.

No tossing in sweaty sheets.
I won't get up to snack, pace, read
or write myself out of insomnia.

No need to count the flock
         of family and friends
who have passed
                    into eternal ethers.

I have Leo's warm skin and kiss,
      lulling me
                  to a sleep deep as his.

Eating the Moon

Three-year-old Leo and I are watching TV.
Blippi, in his striped cap, orange suspenders and bowtie,
dances around the spaceship he built
from cardboard boxes, glitter and paint.

Climbing into its module,
he floats past suspended stars and paper mâché planets
towards a tinfoil moon.

Hours after learning its phases from *Blippi,*
Leo stands on tiptoe, lifting
a large round cookie he christens *full moon*

> Nibbles ...
> Bites ...

Cookie wanes to *half-moon,*
quarter-moon then *oops ...*

Where oh where has the little moon gone?
I sing and pat his belly.

He laughs, now
pointing at the moon he's put back
in the living room window.

Galactic

Blue Haibun

I have the 80-year-old blues. My future has shrunk like the melted candles on my last birthday cake. Knowing my shoes will outlive me, my dress will soon dance alone, I miss my loved ones even when I am with them. But watching a robin perch on my porch railing, I recall her lifespan is five or six years if she's lucky. I have lived to that age at least thirteen times. Half her turquoise eggs will never hatch and most of her chicks will die before they can feather the sky. My middle-aged children fledged long ago and they're banking nest eggs to send their offspring to college. As she warbles her short story in red, green and gold vibrant notes, I still feel blue about fading, but who am I to complain?

A robin's song cheers
the sky. An old rose raises
her head to listen.

Science Lesson

My 8th decade looming, I ask my scientist sweetheart:
After I leave this world, will the universe go on forever?
Please tell me in layman's language.

Pulling our quilt up higher, he enlightens me:
  Some space scholars believe the universe
  will expand so rapidly everything will disintegrate.
  They call it The Big Rip.

I picture my soul as a bedsheet shredded by galactic winds.

  Others believe in the Big Chill.
  Everything will expand so much
  the universe will grow cold and die.

I imagine myself with blue bones too frozen to shiver.

  Then there's the Big Crunch theory.
  Everything stops expanding and collapses
  into a single point that might someday rebound.

I envision my ground-up ashes sucked into a dot
that later explodes into cosmic fireworks.

That's all spectacular, I cry,
but it sounds so unearthly and lonely.
I wish I could be part of the cosmos
in a way that feels human and warm.

  Oh yes you can, he smiles
  melting me with kisses
  till I tumble through glowing darkness
  and see stars on my closed eyelids.

New Lenses

For Jim

Before cataract surgery for both eyes,
you could barely read newspaper print,
the time on your digital watch
or point out behemoth Betelgeuse
sparking Orion's shoulder.

Three weeks after surgery,
instead of a brown blur,
you detail Sonora sand-grains,
fine spines and needles on cacti,
snowflakes lacing the windshield
as you drive through the high sierras.

Worried you'll perceive my coarse pores,
the skein of lines on my brow,
I glow when you reassure me,
You are lovelier than ever.

Your new lenses can't pierce the mist
swaddling the mountains as we snail
along El Mirage trail. Nor can they reflect
the uncharted cosmos, as does the Webb telescope
unfolding gold-coated mirrors.

Celebrating our own miracle
at thanksgiving breakfast,
you marvel at sprinkled sea salt
constellating a fresh-risen loaf.
Surveying a silver fruit platter,
you're awestruck as an astronomer
at the "milky way" white pips on strawberries,
and a blueberry's five-pointed star.

NASA, We Have a Problem!

A partially found poem

Today NASA slams
a spacecraft into an asteroid
at blistering speed, hoping
to alter its orbit
in an unprecedented rehearsal
for the day a killer rock menaces earth.

A climate advisor exults
"those dinosaurs didn't have a space program
to let them know what's coming."

"Woo woo, we have impact,"
planetary defense experts crow
lifting their arms skyward
as telescopes capture it all.

Meanwhile on another news channel,
a leader with ashen hair
cold metallic eyes
and a volcanic will,
aims nuclear words at the world.

Lines in italics are either direct quotes or paraphrased
from a CBC news article, "We have impact!" Sept 26, 2022
https://www.cbc.ca/news/science/asteroid-spacecraft-nasa-dart-1.6596692

Second Chance

If you prick a pinhole
        anywhere
in an image from the Webb Telescope,
    countless galaxies appear,
each one, like our Milky Way,
        smaller than a salt grain
speckling the infinite sky.

Dizzy with wonder
I ponder
        if we burn down our planet,
drown its oceans in trash,
silence the song of its spinning,
or nuke it to nothing,
there might still be a chance
of a duplicate earth
in these gazillion galaxies.

Peopled with cosmic neighbours
peering at us through their scanner,
they might learn to avoid
the course of our own savage saga.

Lilacs Hum in My Garden

I
yearn
for
a
billion
more
bees

enough
balm
to
heal
this
ailing
world

Somewhere

Maybe it's the surprise destination
on the *Spring Blossom Bus Tour* that ends
in a cherry orchard in Belleville
swaying with tipsy bees.

Or the Laurentian meadow
where the stag with a chickadee
perched on one antler grazes.
We pull off the road to look.
My brother says, "Too bad it's a meat farm."
"So much for Eden," I add.

Perhaps it was the river I skated on
holding dad's moonlit hand.

Or the icefloe my children joke
they're going to put me on.

Somewhere could be my home,
the doorbell between my thighs.

It could be a pinhole, black hole,
some parallel universe or multiverse
where my personas can thrive:
cat with nine afterlives.

It's definitely not a cave, crypt or an urn
where I won't wake up to wonder
if *somewhere* is over the rainbow.

Water, Water Everywhere

After a line by Samuel Taylor Coleridge

The surfaces of Pluto and its moon Charon
are frosted as frozen mugs.
Planets Uranus and Neptune
abide in a sea of blue particles.
Due to their hidden water,
the rocks astronauts shunted
back from the moon
are worth more than gold nuggets.

Waiting for my inner supernova:
impending demise,
it comforts me to learn that when
Red Giants explode, they spew
oxygen back into a universe awash
in atoms from which all life is born,
which reminds me

my Mexican grandson, Leo,
named for the constellation,
spoke his first word—
not mama or dada but "Agua"
as he sipped from his cool cosmic cup.

Geocentric

At first earth was a rubber ball bounced against my childhood. It became a grade four geography class globe spun on its axis. In university, I believed the best philosophies came from the ground like carrots. Brian, my tall, well-built brother was nicknamed Orion. I orbited around him but kept my feet on the ground. Later, the planet smelled political. Men died for a patch of soil. Some churches preached those damned souls dwell in earth's core, known as hell. Heaven lay above the clouds. Witches were burned for spelling with pinecones, reading leaves and berries. Today I perceive earth as a blue dot in a pointillist painting called Cosmos. Ideas spill from Mind Dippers and the Milky Way never curdles. I have a universal line and lineage. My DNA might include the gasses around Mother Saturn or dust motes from the breath of Aunt Mars. My stray dog could have been sired by Sirius. No longer geocentric, I am homesick.

Crocheted Constellation

For Helen Louise Vezina

Tonight, in an old Quebec farmhouse
I lie under Helen's constellation
crocheted in less than seven days
by this goddess of bone hooks with yarn
as long as the Saint Lawrence River.

Lacing my fingers through holes
in the fringed afghan,
I draw it over my torso.
Tucking it under my chin, I wonder
if she once slept beneath it
before passing it down to her daughter.

Chain-maker
       Ball-winder
Stitch-saver
       Knot-binder

Did Helen sell other blankets
patterned with a *Milky Way*
to buy fish for her family?
Were her loved ones close-knit?
How did her life unravel?

In the sub-zero dawn
mourning doves huddle
on snow-feathered branches.
Helen's morning stars glow
peach-coloured against my skin.

Galactic Girl

My new tights have a Milky Way pattern.

Their elastic solar system expands as I pull up
my night-sky leggings.

Moons in every size wax and wane on my thighs.

Lepus the hare leaps over my celestial waist.
Capricornus collides with Cetus the whale
whenever I cross my legs.

Saturn spins rings 'round my ankles
and Jupiter sports orange stripes on my skin.

An umbilical string of stars stretches from my navel
and a planet named Earth rests on my belly
as if I'd just given birth.

Narcissa

*After an installation of mirrors and LED lights
by Yayoi Kusama*

All my life I've loved to admire my reflection
in mirrors, windows, potlids and ponds.

Today at the art gallery, I gaze
at my mirrored image multiplied to infinity
on countless suspended
moon-balls and silver planets.

Sharing the artist's faith
in "man's connection with nature",
I cultivate lofty thoughts
about my eternal projection
though sublime creation,
yet worry about my image whirling
through outer space without
a trip to the hairdresser,
a shower, or change of clothes,
like an ungroomed primate.

A few minutes later, rescued by
the timekeeper's bell ushering me
from the exhibit, I wave goodbye
to my cosmic clones
and content myself with a selfie.

Music of Spheres

After Pythagoras

Does it hum like galactic bees,
emit a wind-turbine whine,
or ring supernal chimes ranging
from ephemeral to a sonorous bass?

Perhaps there is a cosmic carousel
where Cetus the whale rides rhythmic soundwaves,
Ursa Major and Minor circle to snow-white noise,
constellation Leo outdoes the MGM roar
in an infinite number of keys.

Maybe the symphonic ether
is scored to swishing comets,
the moon's harmonic tides,
colours of black holes,
chorus of homesick
souls conducted by a creator
with whole notes for eyes.

Whatever its soundscape,
let's pray we don't become so tone deaf,
from mining metallic asteroids,
warring to conquer new spheres,
that we no longer compose hymns to the heavens.

Accompanist

Today my pianist son, James,
whose back curves like a quarter moon
from years bent over the keyboard,
beams full-face.

His two-year-old son, Leo is singing
Twinkle, twinkle little star
                              pitch perfect.

When James tests his range
by modulating skyward
        through higher
                              and higher keys
Leo lifts with the melody
on his winged voice.

Dancing

Kim, today my Mexican daughter-in-law
is teaching me to salsa in my living room.
I think of you in Cuba, fifteen years ago.
Wild about salsa,
you practiced with a passion
hotter than *Habanero Chilli*
or *Camarones a la Diabla*.

Like me, you struggled with basic steps
          pausing on beats four and eight,
   swinging your hips
       as your feet shifted weight.
Later, learning combos and circular patterns,
you mastered multiple Spot Turns
      and seven ways to hold hands.

I dance in memory of you, Kim.

I'm sipping a mojito in *Santa Maria del Mar*,
    lauding you in Latin dance shoes
with suede soles and flared heels,
      free spinning
in our damp, dimly lit
    Russian Resort "ballroom"
to a recording by *La Cara Band*.

Now, may you salsa with souls of legendary singers
   on an ephemeral stage
     where you'll circle the stars.

May you open your arms, inviting us
    to dance with you through the cosmos.

After Looking at Photos
from the Webb telescope

Walking the dog today, I notice
galaxies everywhere—

Flaxen stars sprinkle the neighbor's doormat.

Butterflies sport polka dot planets on their wings.
Ants carry miniscule larvae
through dark holes in their hills
and snails inch across
the lunar-like Arizona landscape.

Constellations of sun-coloured blossoms
grace Palo Verde trees,
and seed-rattling Mesquite pods
mimic the music of spheres.

"We see through a glass darkly …" Saint Paul wrote.
But now we see through better lenses
that pierce the infrared haze to reveal
hidden galaxies. Space prophets predict
that after our lives brief as fireflies,
our dust will form infant stars
gazed at by new generations.

As I clean the dog's sandy paws, I wonder:
do we glimpse our lot clearest of all
when we peer at the ground
and wriggle our dusty bare toes?

Epilogue

Seventy-five years later, marvelling at the star-speckled sky, the Catholic child in me still wonders if there is a heaven. If so, might my sons visit me daily so I wouldn't feel lonely as the last autumn leaf? Would my long-distance lover marry me for eternity? Of course, I'd pray for our hands to stop burning and bleeding our planet. I'd want everyone to sleep in a bed instead of a gutter or sidewalk and to feast in a world at peace. But, knowing the pull of duende—if I dwelled in perpetual bliss, I'd miss eating dinner in front of TV, thrilling to spine-chilling news and pondering the why of evil. I'd long for the tightrope and circus, the smell of shit and temptation, the hooks and claws of creation. The raw fear of dying gnaws my bones and dogs my sleep. But without it, would I treasure my tarnish, love a chipped pinecone or pebble, embrace imperfect people? Yes, I would grow homesick in heaven for this flawed, blessed earth.

Notes

p. 2 Under the Same Roof: The paintings referred to are Marc Chagall's *The Concert* and *The Bride and Groom in the Eiffel Tower.*

p. 3 Fragments: was inspired by *Silica Garden*, created by the founder of 1001 Pots, annual ceramics exhibit in Val David, Quebec.

p. 4 The Apple Gatherer: Helen McNicoll was a Canadian impressionist painter, 1879-1915.

p. 7 Crewel Work Bed Curtain: was shown at *Making Her Mark,* A History of Women Artists in Europe, 1400-1800, AGO exhibit, 2024.

p. 38 Handmaidens, 1955: Catholic nunneries usually "requested" a dowry in exchange for accepting the daughters. Maniple: a vestment worn by a priest celebrating the Eucharist, consisting of a strip hanging from the left arm. Paten: a plate held under the chins of communicants to catch a falling host.

Acknowledgments

These poems, or earlier versions of them, were published in the following literary journals:

"After Looking at Photos Through the Webb Telescope" and "Science Lesson" were published in *Moss Piglet, Outer Space Issue*, 2022.

"After Reading Nobel Prize Winning Poets" appeared in *Moss Piglet, Being Green Issue,* Wisconsin, April 2024.

"Astrid's Ark" appeared in *The Avenue Journal*, Watertower Press, (water theme), Baltimore, Maryland, USA.

"Birdshot" was published in *Women, Life, Freedom Anthology,* edited by Bano Zann and Cy Strom, Guernica, Toronto, 2024.

"Crewel Work Bed Curtain" and "Enough" were published in *The Charleston Anvil*, West Virginia, USA, 2025.

"Dancing" was published in *The Uninvited Season*, an anthology of tribute poems for Kim Grove, Wet Ink Books, 2025.

"Handmaidens, 1955" was first published in *Brimming*, by Donna Langevin, Piquant Press, 2019.

"Homesick in Miami" appeared in *Creation Magazine, Homesick* issue #4, Jan. 2024.

"I Am Susanna Moodie" was published in *The Bridge Newspaper,* edited by Andre Bermon, vol. 4, Issue 4, May 2023.

"If I Were a House", "What I Love About You" and "Circle" won honourable mentions in *The Love Book Anthology*, Blue Cedar Press, Wichita, Kansas, 2024.

"In the Forest of the Night" appeared in *Wordpeace*, Summer/Fall 2022 issue, Lori Desrosiers, Editor/Publisher.

"Maid" was published by *Periwinkle Pelican Lit.* Issue 2, "The Truth Is I Want to Live." USA, 2024.

"Nassau, We Have a Problem" and "Water Water Everywhere" won honouable mention in the *Across the Universe* contest, The Ontario Poetry Society, 2023.

"Neighbour" appeared in *The Bridge Newspaper,* edited by Andre Bermon, Toronto, Sept. 2024.

"No Room Left" Eleven of these poems (or earlier versions of them) in the first part of this section were published in *Homeless City*, a chapbook co-authored by Donna Langevin and Kate Rogers, Aeolus House, 2024.

"Nocturnal" appeared in *Vocivia Magazine*, Issue Five, *Nightmares and Daydreams*, 2024.

"Non-Combustible" appeared in *Agapanthus, Hearth and Home* issue, USA, 2022.

"Ode to Park Benches" was first published in *Peregrine*, 2025 (Amherst Writers and Artists Press). "New Lenses" also appeared in this issue.

"Rehearsal" was published in *Poetry Pause*, the League of Canadian Poets, Nov. 4, 2022.

"Revisiting the House on Hart Street" was published in *inScribe,* Australia, Sept. 2023.

"Science Lesson" and "After Looking at Photos from the Webb Telescope" were first published in *Moss Piglet, Outer Space* Issue, Nov. 2022, Wisconsin, then later won honourable mention in the *Across the Universe* chapbook contest, The Ontario Poetry Society, 2024.

"Somewhere" was published in the *Orenaug Mountain Poetry Journal, (Place theme)*, Oct. 25, 2024.

"The Apple Gatherer" was published in the *Splendor of Wings Anthology,* The League of Canadian Poets, 2024.

"The Gleaner" won Honourable Mention and "Ode to Elation" won Judge's Choice in the *Dr. Henry Drummond Spring Pulse* poetry competition/chapbook, 2024.

"Under the Same Roof" won Honourable Mention in the *Dr. Henry Drummond Spring Pulse* poetry competition/chapbook, 2023.

Thank You to

Those Who Helped Me Build My "House of Poems"

Richard Grove / Tai, my publisher for his decades of friendship, support and faith in my work.

Tom Gannon Hamilton, my musical editor who taught me that the fine art of building a poem begins with a solid foundation, then crafting each line till it sings.

Kate Marshall Flaherty was always ready for a "trade" and helped me to open "windows" to let more light into my poems and enlarge the view.

The members of Kate Marshall Flaherty's *StillPoint* Editing Circle whose input helped improve my construction and decor.

James Dewar's *Crafting Poems* workshops which inspired my two Susanna Moodie monologues, "Hark", "Ode to Elation" and "Enough."

Kate Rogers for some much-appreciated renovations.

Linda Cassidy and James Comeaux for helping me nail some lines.

Seymour Skye for his artful house, made from books instead of bricks, that graces my cover.

Brenda Clews for the author photo that could adorn any wall.

About the Author

Poet/playwright Donna Langevin is a retired ESL teacher and the mother of three sons. The latest of her six poetry collections include *Timed Radiance*, Aeolus House 2022 and *Brimming,* Piquant Press 2019. Appearing in journals in Canada, Australia, India, Israel and the USA, she won second prize in the 2014 GritLIT contest, first prize in the Banister Anthology Competition 2019, and first place in the Ontario Poetry Society Pandemic Poem contest, 2020. Her plays, *Man with the Butterfly Hat, If Socrates Were in My Shoes* and *Remember Him Chasing Squirrels*, were produced at the Toronto Alumnae Theatre NIF Festival in 2015, 2018 and 2020. Winner of a second place Stella Award from Act II Studio, *Summer of Saints* (about the 1847 typhus epidemic) was produced at the Fresh Picks: Sandra Kerr New Plays Festival in 2022. A memoir/fictoire, *A Story for Sadie* was published by Piquant Press in 2023. *Homeless City,* a chapbook co-authored with Kate Rogers, was launched in January 2024 by Aeolus House.

Photo by Brenda Clews

www.ingramcontent.com/pod-product-compliance
Lightning Source LLC
Chambersburg PA
CBHW021122130626
46554CB00002B/820